What is Dying?

Bishop Brent

What is Dying?

Illustrated by Ben Ecclestone

SOUVENIR PRESS

A ship sails
And I stand watching

Til she fades on the horizon,

And someone says:
"She is gone".

Gone where?
Gone from my sight, that is all;

She is just as large as when I saw her

The diminished size
And total loss of sight is in me,
Not in her

And just at the moment
When someone says "she is gone"

There are others

Who are watching her coming
And other voices take up a glad shout

"There she comes"

And that is dying.

Afterword

'What is Dying?' has comforted those who have lost loved ones for nearly a century. Yet, there is no agreement on who actually wrote this remarkable poem. Its message of hope, of the new journey your loved one has gone on, speaks so powerfully that the poem has inspired several writers to publish versions of it.

The most popular version is that of Bishop Charles Henry Brent. Charles Brent was a Missionary Bishop for the Episcopal Church. He came to prominence after being appointed Missionary Bishop of the Philippines in 1902, and devoted himself to establishing Christian communities among the non-Christians of his diocese. Notably, he began a campaign against the opium trade and was instrumental in the creation of several international commissions devoted to destroying international trade in narcotics.

During World War One Bishop Brent served as the Senior Chaplain for the American Armed Forces in Europe and after the war worked to establish a new unity among all Christian denominations, and organised the first World Conference on Faith and Order in 1927.

'What is Dying?' has come to be an inspiration for those who have been left behind when their loved ones depart, it speaks of acceptance and of the certainty of reunion. Despite the uncertainty as to its author 'What is Dying?' speaks movingly and directly with the voice of faith that sustains during a time of grief.

More inspirational books from SOUVENIR PRESS

WEEP NOT FOR ME
By Constance Jenkins
Illustrated by Pat Schaverien

DEATH IS NOTHING AT ALL
By Canon Henry Scott Holland
Illustrated by Paul Saunders

DO NOT STAND AT MY GRAVE AND WEEP
Anonymous
Illustrated by Paul Saunders

REMEMBER ME WHEN I AM GONE AWAY
By Christina Rosetti
Illustrated by Sam Denley

NO MAN IS AN ISLAND
By John Donne
Illustrated by Helen Lush

FRIENDSHIP
By Ralph Waldo Emerson
Illustrated by Richard Allen

WARNING; When I am an Old Woman I Shall
Wear Purple
By Jenny Joseph
Illustrated by Pythia Aston-Jewell

THE DESIDERATA OF HAPPINESS
By Max Ehrmann
Illustrated by Paul Saunders

I CANNOT LIE BY YOUR FIRE
By Robinson Jeffers
Illustrated by Nick Bland

ISBN 0 285 63686 3

Printed in Singapore